q

A Portrait of Liverpool

The Paintings of Allan P. Tankard

© The Bluecoat Press 2006

Published by The Bluecoat Press, Liverpool
Book design by MARCH Graphic Design Studio, Liverpool
Printed by GZ Printek

ISBN 1 904438 45 8

I would like to thank David Tankard, the son of A.P. Tankard now
living in Australia for his help in providing biographical information
about his father and also for his permission to reproduce the
photograph of the Tankard family and the panorama of Liverpool, both
in his possession; also to Sarah Carey, A.P.'s grand daughter who
introduced me to Elizabeth Tankard several years ago. All the other
pictures reproduced in this book are from the collection in Liverpool
Record Office, Central Library, William Brown Street and my thanks
are due to David Stoker, the manager, for permission to use them and
all my former colleagues there. Thanks also to Liverpool John Moores
University for allowing me to consult to the archives of the Liverpool
College of Art. Finally thanks to my ever patient husband.

A PORTRAIT OF LIVERPOOL

THE PAINTINGS OF ALLAN P. TANKARD

Kay Parrott

The Bluecoat Press

In July 1947, 'The Liverpolitan' magazine stated that the Liverpool public had "discovered a man fully equipped to record their city in a way that they could recognise it. An artist who was not offering them his reaction to the place, but one who was interested in the facts themselves". This artist was Allan Peel Tankard, who produced a series of views of the city of Liverpool in the decade after World War II. They show the devastating effects of German bombing raids, particularly on the city centre, but also some of the gems of Liverpool's architecture, which survived the war only to succumb to the redevelopment plans of later years. This book celebrates Tankard's work and is illustrated with pictures from the collection in Liverpool Record Office, in the Central Library, William Brown Street.

CONTENTS

ALLAN PEEL TANKARD

The artist Allan Peel Tankard, through his topographical views in the 1940s and 1950s, is closely associated with the city of Liverpool. However he was actually born in the Hulme district of Manchester on 26th February 1897. His father, also Allan Peel Tankard, a 'master fancy baker' and his wife Edith (formerly Holt) lived at 13 Gloucester Place. The family moved to Liverpool in 1916 when A.P. Tankard senior found employment as a ship's steward. A.P. junior transferred from Manchester College of Art to Liverpool College of Art as a pupil teacher. It appears that he returned briefly to Manchester in November 1921 to complete his training as Liverpool were unable to offer a course on the Theory and Practice of Art Teaching, a subject which would involve Tankard for the rest of his working life. By September the next year he had returned to Liverpool and the College of Art, living at 42 Douglas Road, Anfield and was appointed to the post of Teacher of Still Life and Painting and Drawing from the Antique.

Liverpool College of Art had its origins in the Liverpool Mechanics School of Arts founded in 1825, which had premises in Mount Street in what would later become Liverpool Institute High School for Boys and is now the Liverpool Institute of Performing Arts. In the 1870s the School of Art moved to a new building next door, on the corner of Hope Street, and an extension opened in 1910. In 1905 management was transferred to Liverpool City Council and emphasis shifted away from 'fine arts' and acknowledged the increased importance of applied arts. This was partly influenced by the work of William Morris, but also by the need to make the college more relevant to a wider range of students now that it was under municipal control. By the 1920s the college offered courses in subjects as diverse as design for stage scenery and costumes, wallpaper, furniture and advertising, artistic crafts such as jewellery, lacemaking, illuminating and batik, and artistic trades including furniture making, printing and bookbinding. More traditional courses such as landscape and portrait painting also continued. From just 870 students in the 1920s the college had expanded to 2,632 in 1949/50, a large proportion of whom attended part-time courses. In 1970 the College of Art combined with the College of Building, the College of Commerce and the College of Technology to form

Opposite. A.P. Tankard and his wife, Elizabeth, seen here on their wedding day, July 1938. They are both standing in the centre at the back.

Liverpool Polytechnic, which, in turn has become Liverpool John Moores University.

In the 1920s the college wanted to establish an Art Teaching Certificate course to train new art teachers. Tankard, as previously mentioned, had to return to Manchester to study such a course and he, naturally, became involved. Although numbers were small the course was first offered in 1928/29 and taught by Tankard, virtually single-handed, up to World War II. By 1933 it had evolved to become the Art Teacher's Diploma, in salary terms of degree-equivalent status and Tankard's own salary, second only to those of the Principal and Vice-principal, reflected the status of the course. In 1935, indicating his personal commitment to his work, Tankard presented his own collection of books to form the nucleus of an Art Teaching Department Library. At the end of World War II he was called upon to supervise teacher training to cope with an expected influx of ex-servicemen and by 1950/51 there were 46 students in the department.

In his teaching he wanted his students to be in contact with the world outside the college and he took them to visit other educational establishments, as well as commercial and industrial premises, in search of inspiration. His topographical watercolours of the city probably first date from the late 1940s, when he would take students out to do drawings and watercolours of the bomb damaged city. By the late 1950s students and their approach to their studies were changing and Tankard withdrew from lecturing. "The arrival on the course of a new generation of students created an oil and water situation ... [and he] displayed a sublime unawareness that the world was changing." When he retired in 1961, after forty five years, "there were few who could remember the college without him" and at 6ft 4ins tall, with a deep bass voice, his must have been a distinctive presence.

At the age of 41, on 25th July 1938, A.P. Tankard married Elizabeth Davies at All Saints Church, Stoneycroft. She was 21 years his junior, the daughter of local blacksmith James Davies, and a student studying Drawing and Painting at the College. By this time he had moved from Anfield to 207 Thomas Lane, Broadgreen and Elizabeth lived not far away at 9 Glen Road, off Broadgreen Road. After their marriage they moved to 14 Barmouth Road, Wallasey, where he lived for the rest of his life. Many years later she would assert that he only married her for her cooking, but there must obviously have been more to it than that. Their honeymoon was spent in Prague, however this was not quite the romantic destination it appeared. When they arrived at the station to catch their train they were greeted by students from the college who were to accompany them, for this was a student trip, not a romantic honeymoon for two.

They had two sons, David and Robin. David has vivid memories of accompanying his father on painting expeditions, to places such as Walton. A.P. would suddenly demand water for washing brushes and mixing paints and David, aged eight or nine, would be sent off to find some – not an easy task. It was not until some years later that he felt able to tell his father that the water had come from the local gents' toilet – the only immediately available source! On another occasion he was nearly arrested as a German spy when painting on the beach at Leasowe, when he inadvertently depicted some military installation. Only the intervention of the local mayor, a personal friend, prevented him from being locked up.

Tankard did not enjoy a long retirement. He died in November 1964, only three years after leaving the College of Art. He often used to sketch fellow train travellers, usually pretty girls to the embarrassment of his young son, and even when he was in hospital he continued to draw, in this case pictures of the nurses. The Liverpool Daily Post at the time of his death said that "in the last twenty five years [he] has immortalised the changing face of Liverpool."

In this book Tankard's work in depicting post-war Liverpool is celebrated, but he also visited and painted other places. In his youth he visited France and Yugoslavia, during World War II he painted in Wales and in 1945 he spent ten days in Lapland. His Liverpool views are line and wash drawings, but he also worked in other media, such as oils and sculpture and produced portrait and abstract paintings. His topographical views were painted mainly from observation, sometimes from memory, and had numerous reference sketches on the walls of his studio. He completed his pictures quickly, preferably when the sun was shining, which he said made the buildings 'sparkle.'

The Liverpolitan, July 1947.

RECORDING MERSEYSIDE

In February 1945 a number of local artists, including Tankard, were asked to submit pictures, in any medium except oils, of various local architectural subjects for an exhibition to be held later that year entitled 'Recording Merseyside.' The objective of the exhibition was to stimulate interest in the city and the surrounding area's architectural heritage. The subjects selected were included on the government's scheme for Air Raid Damage to Buildings of Historic Interest or the National Buildings Record. All the subjects dated back to at least 1850, in itself a reflection of the architectural taste of the time. The exhibition ran at the Bluecoat Chambers from October 8th to November 10th 1945 and there was extensive coverage in the local press with the Liverpool Daily Post publishing the exhibition catalogue. It turned out to be the most successful small exhibition of art held in the city and two further exhibitions on the same theme were held in 1946 and 1947. Twenty seven pictures by various artists were acquired by Liverpool Libraries to add to their collection of mostly nineteenth century topographical watercolours, 21 of which were purchased at a cost of £319 14s 0d.

Tankard contributed nine of the 83 pictures in the exhibition and his subjects ranged from street scenes, such as Rodney Street, Dale Street and Bold Street, to buildings including the Town Hall, the Government Offices in Victoria Street and Leyland's Bank in King Street. In the catalogue the prices for his pictures ranged from 5 guineas (for a pencil sketch) to 18 guineas. Tankard continued to exhibit his views of Liverpool locally, for example at an exhibition of 'Watercolours by Local Artists' at the Bluecoat Chambers in July 1949. In 1950 two of his pictures were selected for exhibition at the Royal Academy in London, a view of Rodney Street and one of Ranelagh Street from the bombed Lewis's store. In 1951 two of Tankard's pictures of Liverpool were sent to Berlin. One was presented to the Mayor of Berlin and the other to the King's (Liverpool) Regiment, stationed in the city at that time. He also received commissions from banks and breweries for views of their premises.

Liverpool Libraries continued to purchase his watercolours in the late 1940s and early 1950s. There are no references to commissions in the Libraries, Museums and

Arts Committee Minute Books for these dates, so it is not clear if the subjects were chosen by J.F. Smith, the City Librarian, or the artist himself. Several pictures were usually purchased each month, at prices ranging from five to sixteen guineas and eventually the Record Office in the Central Library acquired about 200 of his views. The majority are of streets around the city centre, especially Lime Street, Church Street, Renshaw Street, Mount Pleasant and Ranelagh Street. There are a number of views of Knotty Ash and Broadgreen, where he lived prior to his marriage and also some of nineteenth century merchants' villas in the suburbs. Perhaps surprisingly there are no pictures in the collection of some of Liverpool's most famous buildings, the Liver Building, the Mersey Docks and Harbour Board offices and the Cunard Building at the Pier Head or St George's Hall, although they may appear in the distance.

POST-WAR LIVERPOOL

The damage suffered by Liverpool during World War II is evidence of the importance the enemy placed on the city as a special target, both for its strategic position controlling the Atlantic and the Western Approaches, and also as the country's second port. Between August 1940 and August 1942 the city suffered 90 air attacks in which 4,000 people were killed. In the May Blitz of 1941 alone 1,300 died, 6,585 homes were destroyed, 125,310 properties were seriously damaged, including many important public and commercial buildings. There was massive damage to the docks and the city centre, which was described at one point as "a raging inferno of fire." The area to the south of Lord Street and east of Paradise Street was devastated. A famous photograph taken from the Victoria Monument at the top of Lord Street, which was unscathed, shows the scale of the destruction, with scarcely a building standing. The city's greatest loss was the Custom House, severely damaged and later demolished. Other buildings such as the Central Library and Museum and the Bluecoat Chambers were badly damaged but rebuilt. Both Lewis's and Blackler's department stores were also hit and rebuilt on the same sites. However St George's Hall, the Town Hall, the still unfinished Anglican Cathedral and the waterfront buildings at the Pier Head escaped serious damage.

The next 35 years saw a massive rebuilding process, summarised by the City Council as "Repair, Renewal, Removal and Reorganisation." Housing was seen as the most important priority. Before the war Liverpool already had a huge housing problem, with a shortage of suitable quality housing and the legacy of the Victorian slums. This was, of course, exacerbated by the loss of so much housing stock in bombing raids. There was also a vast backlog of routine maintenance, which had virtually ceased during the war on houses and other buildings. But building was restricted by a shortage of materials and strict government controls, giving each local authority a quota for new house starts. In the 1950s and 1960s the Council implemented a policy of dispersing people from poor quality housing in the inner areas to large new council estates, such as Kirkby, Speke and Halewood, on the outskirts of the city. This provided new, better quality housing, but also broke up established communities and changed the character of the city. As well as more and better housing, the city needed new buildings for education, social welfare and employment, but the change from a wartime to a peacetime economy could not be achieved overnight. Temporary wartime building works had to be removed; public shelters had been built for 82,000 and there were domestic shelters for 700,500 people and initially only essential work could be undertaken. Work on the first new school did not start until 1947 and rebuilding the Central Library had to wait until 1957.

In the 1950s the docks were busy again and they were still the largest local employer, although the number of jobs had started to decline. In this decade an attempt was made to diversify the city's economic basis from its former reliance on the docks and associated trades. Previously any manufacturing which existed, such as Tate and Lyle's sugar refinery and the Rank flour mills, had a close relationship with the port. Industrial estates were established, at for example Speke and Aintree, where the Corporation built and leased factory units to firms such as food processors, electrical engineers and printers. Gradually as unemployment decreased the standard of living improved and people started to acquire consumer goods such as refrigerators, washing machines and even cars.

According to Joseph Sharples in the new Pevsner guide to Liverpool "with hindsight wartime bomb damage was less destructive than the subsequent efforts of architects and planners". St John's Market and the surrounding area were demolished in the 1960s to make way for a shopping centre and a similar fate befell Clayton Square in the 1980s. Fortunately some ambitious redevelopment plans came to nothing. The Liverpool City Centre Plan published in 1965 declared two thirds of the city centre obsolete and advocated wholesale demolition to construct a new road network, preserving just a few notable buildings. There were also proposals for a massive civic centre on the site of St John's Gardens, equal in conception and scale to anything in Communist East Europe.

The post-war years are depicted in A.P. Tankard's watercolours reproduced in this book, showing the damage caused during World War II and the city waiting for the process of rebuilding and reinvigoration to begin.

City Panorama

This magnificent panoramic view of central Liverpool appears to have been taken from a vantage point somewhere near Lime Street Station. In the bottom left-hand corner is Lewis's department store, with famous statue by Jacob Epstein, and the Lyceum at the bottom of Bold Street. Continuing clockwise the buildings include the Bluecoat Chambers, where Tankard had his studio, the Sailors' Home in Canning Place, the Mersey Docks and Harbour Board building and the Liver Building, at the Pier Head. At the centre top is Martin's Bank Building, with Exchange Flags to its right and the Municipal Buildings and Town Hall in front. On the extreme right are the Museum and the Central Library, and Gerard Gardens flats behind, with the Wellington Monument and the North Western Hotel at the bottom right, in front of the station. In the centre is St George's Hall, with the entrance to the Queensway Tunnel beyond and St John's Market, the Playhouse theatre and Clayton Square to the left.

TOWARDS THE RIVER

Goree Piazzas, c.1948

Despite their somewhat exotic name these were, in fact, part of a large series of warehouses, named after the island of Goree off the West African coast where slaves were assembled for transportation, and built by the Corporation in 1793 behind the then George's Dock. The buildings were all destroyed by a fire in 1803, so fierce that it was reported to have burned for three months. The warehouses were rebuilt in the early nineteenth century, six storeys high and with a street level stone arcade, the Goree Piazzas, for pedestrians, similar to an Italian square. They were once again severely damaged, by bombing in World War II and the remains can be seen here, just prior to their final demolition, with the Liver Building in the background.

Binns Collection C203

Canning Place, 1948

This is the south side of Canning Place, from Mersey Street on the left to Wapping. Canning Place was the site of Liverpool's first dock, the Old Dock, which opened in the early eighteenth century, but which a century later had became too small and congested to deal with the number of ships using the port. The Old Dock closed in 1826 and new docks were developed on land to the west, reclaimed from the river. However the site provided an ideal location for a new Custom House of suitable size and importance to reflect Liverpool's status as a growing port, and this opened in 1839. The public house in the centre is aptly named the Custom House Hotel. *Binns Collection C216.*

Custom House, 1947

This is Liverpool's 5th Custom House, in Canning Place, designed by John Foster, the Town Surveyor and built between 1828 and 1839 on the site of the town's first dock. As well as a Custom House and Excise Office the building included a Post Office and Telegraph Office (open 24 hours a day) and the offices of the Mersey Docks and Harbour Board. It was vast; the principal north front, seen here facing Castle Street, was 470 feet long and the 'Long Room' occupying the centre of the building was 145 feet long, 60 feet wide and 40 feet high. However the building sustained serious damage during the May Blitz, as can be seen here and in the 1950s the controversial decision was made to demolish what remained. *Binns Collection D422*

19

Canning Place, 1948

This view shows numbers 2 to 10 Canning Place, from Strand Street on the left to Litherland Alley on the right, with Crooked Lane in the centre. From left to right the properties are: the Mersey Transport Café and hostel, Irlam Insecticides, Gamon Arden and Co, solicitors and Diocesan Registry for Marriage Licences, E.H. Jones Ltd., paint manufacturers (Stanley Paint Works), Fenton Bros., rubber goods manufacturers, Arvon Chambers and Harold A. Fenton, coffee house proprietor.

Binns Collection C206

Strand Street, 1948

Strand Street, just around the corner from the previous picture, numbers 25 to 31, but the property is in a somewhat derelict state, with windows boarded up and holes in the roofs. As its name implies Strand Street was the original shoreline of the River Mersey. All the land to the west, on which Canning, Albert, George's and the other docks were built, was reclaimed from the river. *Binns Collection C211*

Strand Street, 1948

This is the other end of Strand Street, from James Street to Redcross Street, in the centre, with the 'Trawler' public house, proprietor D. George Regan, on the extreme right. The building occupied by the Harwol Specialities Company is derelict and has been boarded up, presumably following bomb damage. John Taylor, marine engineer, had premises on the opposite corner of Redcross Street.
Binns Collection C213

Mersey Street, 1948

Mersey Street runs south from Canning Dock, emerging on Wapping via Salthouse Lane, close to Salthouse Dock. At number 17, on the right, are the premises of Thomas Ollis and Co., printers' engineers. Many of the other premises are occupied by trades with a maritime connection; the United Africa Co. Ltd., African merchants; Wilson, Vosper and Coltart, ships stores dealers; James Chambers and Co., sailmakers; Abel Foxall and Sons, chain manufacturers. *Binns Collection C212*

Hurst Street, 1948

Hurst Street is the continuation of Mersey Street and here we are looking south, at its junction with Salthouse Lane, with the premises of J.S. Quine and Sons, shipsmiths, in the centre.

This was an area of warehouses and a number of paint manufacturers, including J. and W. Wilson Ltd. and H. Davison and Sons Ltd. Horsepower was obviously still in use, as shown by the horse and cart turning into Salthouse Lane and also the cart parked on the left. *Binns Collection C214*

24

King Street, 1945

Most of the pictures in this book are watercolours, but this pencil sketch shows the bombed remains of Leyland's Bank which stood at the corner of King Street and South John Street, close to Canning Place. The bank was founded in the early years of the nineteenth century by Thomas Leyland, Liverpool's first millionaire and three times mayor, whose wealth was founded on a lottery win, as well as connections with privateering and the slave trade. The bank moved to its premises in King Street in 1815 and remained there until World War II. The area is now the site of the new Grosvenor shopping centre. *Local Collection 299*

Sea Brow, 1948

Sea Brow was a short street, which ran from James Street to Redcross Street, parallel to Strand Street. As can be seen from the damaged buildings and empty spaces, this area suffered extensive bomb damage. However some businesses are still trading, including F.J. Callaghan and Co., ships' furnishers and F.A. Jones Ltd., engineers' merchants, in the red painted building, and beyond that, the Dominion Tea Plantation Co Ltd. and the Red Lion Hotel.

Binns Collection C215

James Street Station,
Liverpool Overhead Railway, 1957

Liverpool's Overhead Railway, known locally as the 'Dockers' Umbrella', ran immediately behind the Pier Head buildings, which can be seen here, together with the George's Dock Ventilation and Control Station. This contained offices and part of the ventilation system for the Queensway (old) Mersey Tunnel. An overhead railway had first been suggested in 1853, as a means of relieving congestion in the area of the docks, but the new railway, for passengers only, did not open until 1893. After its extension in 1896 it ran for seven miles from the Dingle, in the south, to Seaforth Sands, in the north.

Local Collection 514

**Pier Head Station,
Liverpool Overhead Railway, 1957**

There were 14 stations on the railway, some of which, as can be seen in these pictures, were very close together. It was constructed as an iron viaduct, supported on iron columns, some of which had to be embedded in warehouses or the boundary walls of existing buildings. Prefabricated sections were brought along the already built deck and lowered into position by a gantry, which would then be moved along ready for the next section.

Local Collection 513

Custom House Station,
Liverpool Overhead Railway, 1957

With superb views along the whole length of Liverpool's docks, the Overhead Railway soon became a tourist attraction, where passengers could view shipping from all over the world. However by 1954, after 60 years of exposure to salt-laden air and neglect during World War II, an estimated £2 million of urgent repairs were needed to keep the railway operational. Sadly this amount was beyond the resources of the Liverpool Overhead Railway Company and it closed on 30 December 1956. These views appear to have been painted after its closure, but before demolition work had started.

Local Collection 515

THE BUSINESS AREA

Town Hall, 1950

An unusual view over the roof of the Town Hall, looking south-east from the top of the Exchange, with the Anglican Cathedral in the distance. This is Liverpool's third Town Hall; built to the designs of John Wood of Bath, it opened with a week of festivities in 1754. The building was severely damaged by fire in January 1795 and after reconstruction by James Wyatt, the dome and cupola with the statue of Minerva on the top, were added in 1802. *Binns Collection B92*

Exchange Buildings, 1950

Liverpool's first Exchange, specifically built to provide accommodation for the town's merchants, was constructed in the early nineteenth century, built round a quadrangle at the rear of the Town Hall. As trade grew during the century it became obvious that another, larger building was needed and a new Exchange, designed by T.M. Wyatt, opened in 1867 on the same site. This building was, in its turn, replaced and work on the third Exchange started in the 1930s. However by the start of World War II in 1939, only the first phase had been completed and the apparently damaged area of the old building to the left may be due to interrupted demolition rather than bomb damage.

Binns Collection C276

Albert Lambert
October 1950

Exchange Buildings, 1950

This is a close-up view of the arcade in the old Exchange, showing the corner in the left of the previous picture. The architectural style was described by Picton as "a sort of Flemish Renaissance" and the building cost £220,000. Divided into numerous rooms for individual traders, it was effectively a large office block, with the added facility of a newsroom. In 1938 the newsroom was taken over by the Admiralty as the Western Approaches Headquarters during the war. *Binns Collection C275*

Chapel Street, c.1950

This view of Chapel Street, looking west from Tithebarn Street towards the river, shows both the old and new Exchange buildings. On the left the 1860s building is supported by scaffolding, awaiting demolition and beyond, dwarfing the previous building, is the part-completed new Exchange, not finished until 1955. The distinctive tower of St Nicholas' Church can be seen in the distance. *Binns Collection C277*

Water Street, 1947

Water Street runs from the Town Hall, at its junction with Castle Street, down to the River Mersey. Here the distant view is dominated by the Liver Building, and the Overhead Railway can be seen crossing Water Street just beyond the trams. This was very much the commercial heart of the city, with offices such as India Buildings, Martin's Bank Buildings, Barclay's Bank Building, Oriel Chambers and New Zealand House. These provided offices for shipowners and agents, solicitors, ship brokers, forwarding agents, colliery agents, accountants and government departments, as well as branches of the various banks.

Binns Collection D434

Oriel Chambers, 1945

Built in 1864 and designed by the Liverpool architect Peter Ellis, this office building was considered revolutionary at the time and described as a "great abortion" when built. It stands at the corner of Water Street and Covent Garden. The framework is cast iron and the façades consist of a series of tall oriel windows. This view shows bomb damage sustained by the Covent Garden front, which was originally twice as long. Today the building is still strikingly modern and it is hard to believe that it was built in the mid-nineteenth century.

Binns Collection C174

Municipal Buildings, Dale Street, 1951

These offices were designed to bring together all the departments of the expanding Corporation in one building. The original design by John Weightman, in a mixture of Italian and French Renaissance styles, was modified by his successor as Corporation surveyor, E.R. Robson and completed in 1867/8. *Binns Collection B93*

Sir Thomas Street, 1951

Sir Thomas Street, originally known as Sir Thomas Buildings, was named after Sir Thomas Johnson, prominent in Liverpool affairs in the early eighteenth century, and building work started in the early years of that century. Like many old Liverpool streets it was narrow and irregular and also liable to flood, so that sometimes the only way across was by boat. In the centre of this view are the City Education Offices, built in the late nineteenth century in "late Gothic – early Renaissance" style and now converted into flats. In the foreground is the balustrade which surrounded the bombed site of the Government Buildings in Victoria Street.

Binns Collection D457

Victoria Street, 1949

Victoria Street was built in 1867/8 through an area of tightly packed courts and yards between Sir Thomas Buildings (now Sir Thomas Street) and Old Haymarket, continuing towards Cook Street. This view, looking south west near the junction with Stanley Street towards Castle Street, is outwardly little changed. On the left were the Fruit Exchange and Produce Exchange Building, with many businesses in the area engaged in related trades. Most of the buildings on Victoria Street were let as offices, with a wide range of businesses, including numerous fruit and provision importers, produce brokers and dried fruit merchants, as well as motor tyre manufacturers, haulage contractors and the intriguing 'India Rubber, Gutta Percha and Telegraph Works Ltd.', rubber goods manufacturers.

Binns Collection C241

39

Victoria Street, 1949

Another view of Victoria Street, but this time looking north-east, with the colonnade of the Picton Library in the distance. The building on the right, where the road narrows, is still there and beyond is the former Head Post Office, which was severely damaged and lost its top two floors during the May Blitz. For many years the area behind the façade was used as a yard for Post Office vans, but has recently been rebuilt as the Met Quarter shopping centre. On the left, between Sir Thomas Street and Crosshall Street, stood Government Buildings, like the Post Office bombed during the May Blitz but subsequently demolished. The area is still empty today and used as a car park. *Binns Collection C242*

Derby Square, 1954

Much of the property to the south of Derby Square was bombed during the war and this view looks across the land which has been cleared and is in use as a car park. The Victoria Monument, which survived the bombing, can be seen on the left. It was built on the site of St George's Church, demolished in 1897 and in turn built on the site of Liverpool Castle. The building on the right was built as the Alliance Bank and became Trials Hotel in the 1980s, with Castle Moat House to its left, built in 1841 for the North and South Wales Bank. The towers of the Liver Building can be seen in the distance. *Binns Collection B103*

41

North John Street, 1947

North John Street and its continuation South John Street, were constructed in the late eighteenth century to provide a through route from north to south and were originally known just as John Street. Like many streets in Liverpool in the early nineteenth century it was very narrow, scarcely wide enough for two carriages to pass each other. In the 1820s John Street was widened at a cost of £32,750, together with Lord Street and other thoroughfares in the centre of town. North John Street is seen here looking from the blitzed area of Lord Street. On the right, at the far end, is the golden dome of the Royal Insurance building, built in grand Neo-baroque style around an innovative self-supporting steel frame, which enabled the architect, J. Francis Doyle, to incorporated a large, column free General Office on the ground floor.

Binns Collection D441

LONDON ROAD
AND WILLIAM BROWN STREET

London Road, 1946

This view of London Road looks west, from its junction with Norton Street, downhill towards Lime Street, with the column of the Wellington Monument in the distance. The Swan Inn is shown here and on the opposite side of the road is the Tudor Restaurant, with Price's Fifty Shilling Tailors next door. The 'Fifty Shilling' referred to the cost of a gentleman's suit and the same firm had another shop further down London Road, as well as one in Lord Street.

Binns Collection D414

Monument Place, 1946

The triangular open space halfway up London Road is known as Monument Place after the equestrian statue of George III commemorating the 50th anniversary of his accession to the throne, sited just to the left of this view. The stone building in the picture, behind the telephone box, is a Post Office. From left to right the other premises are: Whetstone Entertainments Ltd., who ran a dance hall at Orrell Park, Miss Alice Woods, wardrobe dealer, the Royal Liver Friendly Society and Jay's Furnishing Stores, whose premises' extended into Pembroke Place.

Binns Collection D413

Norton Street, 1947

Norton Street is another road which runs from London Road to Islington and here the west side is shown, with the Tudor Restaurant at the junction with London Road. Montague Burton Ltd., tailors, had premises on the opposite corner. Perhaps surprisingly a number of film companies had offices in Norton Street, including Twentieth Century Fox, United Artists, Columbia Pictures, the British Lion Film Corporation as well as the less well known Eros Film Corporation. Today all this property has been demolished and a new coach station stands at the junction of Norton Street and Islington.

Binns Collection D418

St Vincent Street, 1946

St Vincent Street runs south from London Road, at its junction with Norton Street. Today it forms part of the traffic management system around the city centre and most of the property shown here has been demolished. The Swan Inn stood at the junction from at least 1860 and in 1949 the licensee was Ronald John Crossley. Cope Brothers and Co Ltd, the tobacco manufacturers had premises in St Vincent Street, which extended to the adjacent Lord Nelson Street. *Binns Collection D411*

Shakespeare Theatre, 1956

In June 1888 the Shakespeare Theatre in Fraser Street, off London Road, opened with a performance of Shakespeare's "As you like it". One of the most elaborately constructed and best appointed theatres in the country, it was richly decorated in crimson and gold, with stained glass windows, a magnificent foyer with a carved mahogany booking office and marble staircase to the first floor lounge and dress circle. It was also the first theatre in the city to be lit by electric light. Initially built to stage quality drama, its fortunes gradually declined through variety to short-lived theatre club ventures in the 1950s and 1960s. In the 1960s it reopened as the Shakespeare Casino Club until destroyed by fire in March 1976.

Binns Collection C312

London Road, 1946

This view shows London Road, from its junction with Lime Street, on the right, to Pudsey Street. The road was one of the early routes out of Liverpool, leading initially to Warrington and eventually to London. At the end of the eighteenth century there were no houses beyond this point, just fields and a bridleway leading over the gently rising heath. A coaching inn or public house named the 'Legs of Man' stood at the junction of Lime Street and London Road from the late eighteenth century, although rebuilt, until its recent demolition to make way for an extension to the Empire Theatre.

Binns Collection D412

Commutation Row, 1950

Commutation Row, at the top of William Brown Street, was once the site of the "Folly Fair" held annually at Easter time, which reached the height of its popularity towards the end of the eighteenth century. There were temporary theatres, merry-go-rounds, swingboats, gingerbread booths and other stalls. Houses were built on Commutation Row and the name is said to derive from some sort of 'commutation' or exchange in kind made when the land was purchased. The original houses were deliberately built with unusually large windows in an attempt to evade the current window tax, levied according to the number of windows in a house, not their size.

Binns Collection C250

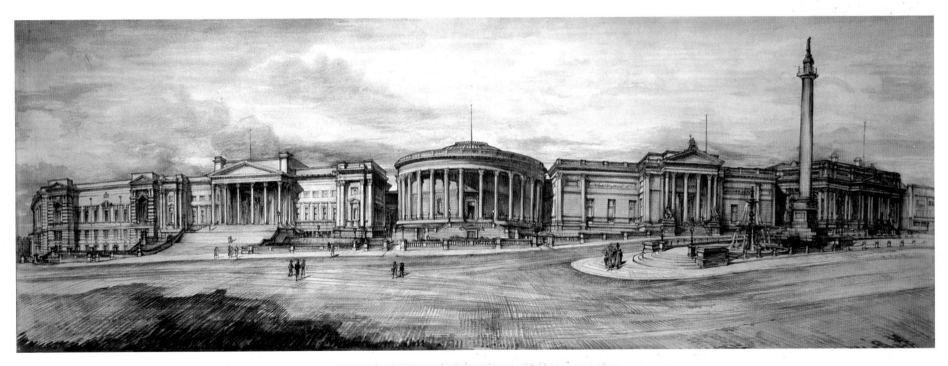

William Brown Street, 1946

This panoramic view of William Brown Street shows the former College of Technology, on the left, now part of the National Museums Liverpool, with the steps of the old museum entrance and the Brown Library to the right. This building was bombed and severely damaged during the May Blitz in 1941 and when this picture was painted the area behind the façade was still awaiting reconstruction. The circular Picton Library, based on the reading room of the old British Museum Library in London, was one of the first buildings in the city to have electric light installed. The next buildings in the row are the Walker Art Gallery, built 1874-7 and paid for by Liverpool's mayor, the brewer Andrew Barclay Walker, and the County Sessions House. In front of these two buildings are the Steble Fountain, the gift of Col. R.F. Steble, and the Wellington Memorial, inaugurated in 1863 and 132 feet high. *Binns Collection A20*

St John's Gardens, 1954

Once the site of St John's Church, which obscured the view of the west side of St George's Hall, St John's Gardens opened in 1904 and provided a site in the city for commemorative statues. In the foreground in this painting is the memorial to the King's Liverpool Regiment, formed in 1685. It commemorates soldiers who died in campaigns in Afghanistan (1878-80), Burma (1885-87) and the Boer War in South Africa (1899-1902). The central figure on the pedestal is Britannia, with a soldier of 1685 on the left and a contemporary soldier of 1902 on the right. The statue to the rear is of William Ewart Gladstone (1809-1898), born in Liverpool and four times Liberal prime minister.

Binns Collection B100

Byrom Street, 1949

The dominant building here is the Liverpool Technical College, opened in 1901. The design for the building was won in competition by E.W. Mountford, and sculptures by F.W. Pomeroy depict a symbolic figure of Liverpool holding a globe and sceptre and Minerva, symbolising wisdom. The upper floors were originally an extension of the museum in William Brown Street, but in 2000/2001 the entire building was refurbished and incorporated into the museum.

Binns Collection D448

Byrom Street, 1949

The Army and Navy Boot Stores (also trading as C.W. Coates and Sons) had a total of four shops on Byrom Street. This picture shows the premises at numbers 22 to 26, between Clayton Street and Cuerdon Street. They are described in Kelly's Liverpool Directory for 1949 as "naval and military outfitters and boot factors" and "government contractors". The building on the left was the Byrom Unique Hostel for men, with the Unique Café, or Tom Smith's Dining Rooms, on the ground floor and had previously been a temperance hotel, with the Popular Café beneath. By 1949 the hostel had moved to Shaw Street, but the name remained on the building. The site is now a car park beneath the Churchill Way flyover. *Binns Collection C232*

54

Hunter Street, 1948

This is the south side of Hunter Street, which ran from Byrom Street to Christian Street and is now the site of the Churchill Way flyover linking Islington with Dale Street and Tithebarn Street. On the left are the premises of the Manchester Slate Co. Ltd. (named here by Tankard as the Monumental Slate Co. Ltd.) and beyond that is the Quaker Meeting House, built in 1796 and replacing their former meeting house in Hackins Hey.
Binns Collection 220

St Stephen Street, 1948

Tankard did not just paint Liverpool's important streets, he also included small, insignificant streets such as this one. By doing so he added greatly to the overall picture of the city at this time. St Stephen's Street ran parallel to Byrom Street, between Hunter Street and Clayton Street and was named after St Stephen's Church. This was built in 1722 as a Baptist Chapel and stood in Byrom Street. The site of the road is now beneath the Churchill Way flyover to Dale Street. The large building at the rear of the street is the Liverpool Technical College, now part of National Museums Liverpool. *Binns Collection D445*

AROUND LIME STREET

Lime Street, 1948

This shows the main entrance to Lime Street Station in 1948, with the North Western Hotel to the left and shops and public houses to the right. This was the terminus of the Liverpool and Manchester Railway, which opened in 1830, although for the first five years of operation trains started and finished at Edge Hill, two miles to the east. The new terminus, in the centre of town, opened in 1836 and occupied the northern part of the present day station. The glazed semi-circular roof span of 200 feet, shown in this view, was constructed in the mid 1880s when the station was expanded to cope with increasing traffic. *Binns Collection C198*

Lime Street, 1948

A view of Lime Street, between Skelhorne Street and Brownlow Hill. The Crown Hotel on the left, completed in 1905, has one of the richest 'Art Nouveau' exteriors in Liverpool, although here it is prominently advertising 'Wills Capstan cigarettes'. Beyond are the Futurist and Scala cinemas, with the bulk of the Adelphi Hotel behind. Lime Street was originally called Limekiln Lane, after the kilns owned by William Harvey, which were situated where Lime Street station is today and removed to the North Shore in 1804, following complaints about the smoke and fumes. First laid out as a road in about 1715, the name was not changed until 1790. There were roperies along Lime Street until 1812, supplying the needs of the increasing number of sailing ships using the port. *Binns Collection C197*

St George's Hall, 1946

This is the south front of St George's Hall, with the North Western Hotel behind and the roof of Lime Street Station to the right. St George's Hall, designed by Harvey Lonsdale Elmes, opened on 18 September 1854 and combined the functions of assize courts and assembly hall. At 490 feet long, its size is almost unique among British secular buildings and it has a central Great Hall, assize courts opening off either end, and a semi-circular concert hall at the north end. Much of the interior decoration is by C.R. Cockerill, who completed work on the hall after the premature death of Elmes in 1847.

Binns Collection D404

Lime Street, 1948

This busy scene shows Lime Street from Hanley Street on the left to Skelhorne Street on the right, adjacent to the Lime Street Station. The 'Savoy' public house is on the left, then to the right the Marigold Milk Bar, W.E. McLachlan, tobacconist, who had a number of shops in Liverpool and the surrounding area, and finally Rene Adair, gowns. Today all these shops in front of the station have gone and have been replaced by a new row of shops, topped by the thirteen storey tower of Concourse House, built in 1967/68. *Binns Collection C204*

St George's Place, 1947

St George's Place is the triangular area, opening off Lime Street, near the south front of St George's Hall and opposite Lime Street Station. In 1949 the row of buildings shown here had a number of hotels and public houses, including the Hotel St George, the Imperial Hotel ("first class family and commercial"), the Douglas Hotel and the Caledonian Vaults. The West Lancashire Territorial and Auxiliary Forces Association had their headquarters in St George's Building (numbers 24 to 32), together with the Liverpool Press Club Ltd and several press photographers. The Territorials' name can be seen on the building, together with advertisements for Lewis's department store and Nicholson's gin. *Binns Collection D419*

62

Lime Street, 1948

A view of Lime Street from the North Western Hotel to Hanley Street. The shops in front of the station included a café/tobacconists, a chemist, a dry cleaners, 'Glad-Wear' costumiers and the 'Sterling Boot Co.' There were also two public houses, the 'Royal Hotel', manager Thomas Henry Dodd, and the 'Savoy' at the opposite corner, licensee Charles Golding. The North Western Hotel, designed by Alfred Waterhouse, opened in 1871. Built of Storeton stone from Bebington, this hotel was designed on a monumental scale, with 7 floors and 330 rooms. Plans to demolish it in the 1970s fortunately came to nothing and it has now been converted into student accommodation for Liverpool John Moores University. *Binns Collection C199*

Lime Street, 1947

This view of Lime Street shows the Vines Hotel, at the junction with Copperas Hill. It was built in 1907 for the Liverpool brewer Robert Cain and designed by Walter W. Thomas, who also produced the Philharmonic Hotel in Hope Street. The interior is as ornate as the exterior, with mahogany and copper fittings, plaster reliefs by the Bromsgrove Guild and Gustave Hiller. In 1949 the licensee was Charles Senar. Further along Lime Street on this side were two cinemas, the Scala and the Futurist, both now closed. *Binns Collection D416*

Lime Street, 1959

This animated scene shows Professor Codman's famous Punch and Judy show in Lime Street, with the North Western Hotel, Lime Street Station and even the Punch and Judy café, just to the right of the tent. At this date the main entrance to the station was on Lime Street. Despite the crowds there is remarkably little traffic and what there is, such as the cars and coach on the right, seems to be moving in strange directions. Note the girl with a 'hula hoop' near the coach. *Local Collection 511*

Elliot Street, 1947

Elliot Street is the short road which runs from the north east end of Clayton Square uphill to Lime Street and St George's Place. This view looks towards Clayton Square. On the left is the curved art-deco façade of the Forum Cinema, designed by William R. Glen and opened in 1931. Beyond, on the same side, is Blackler's department store, which opened in 1908. Blackler's had a reputation for stocking things which other stores did not sell, still offering, for instance, tin baths in the 1970s, and catering for its more senior customers. It was also famous for its Christmas grotto and 20 feet high Father Christmas, which dominated the main staircase in the centre of the shop.
Binns Collection D417

Elliot Street, 1947

This view shows Elliot Street, at its junction with Great Charlotte Street, looking towards Clayton Square. On the left is a branch of the Westminster Bank and St John's Market is on the right. Today all this property has been demolished and St John's Precinct is on the right, with the Clayton Square shopping centre to the left. The sloping road has been made into a flight of steps between the two shopping centres. *Binns Collection D423*

Elliot Street, 1947

In the foreground is Clayton Square, with Elliot Street in the centre, looking towards the Crown Hotel on Lime Street, with Houghton Street to the left. Stalls of flower sellers were always a feature of Clayton Square and they can be seen here plying their trade. Part of the way up Elliot Street, on the left, is St John's Market.

Designed by John Foster and built at a cost of £35,000, the building was completed in 1832. Occupying 2 acres and surrounded on four sides by streets, the simple building provided a large area protected from the weather for a general food market. In the 1960s it was demolished to make way for the new St John's Precinct. Although it lacked modern facilities and had become increasingly insanitary, its replacement is hardly an improvement and today it would probably be retained and refurbished. *Binns Collection D426*

Elliot Street, 1947

This is another view of St John's Market, looking towards Clayton Square. The streets on either side of the market, Great Charlotte Street, to the right and Market Street, on the far side, were occupied by traders in businesses such as florists, fishmongers, fruit merchants and importers, and also bird dealers. Beyond the market is Owen Owen's department store, built on the northern side of Clayton Square in the 1920s to designs by Walter Aubrey Thomas. Originally planned as a hotel, it is now a branch of Tesco Metro. *Binns Collection D429*

CLAYTON SQUARE TO CHURCH STREET

Clayton Square, 1947

Clayton Square is named after Sarah Clayton who, unusually for a woman in the eighteenth century, was a property developer and industrialist. After leasing the land in 1746 and 1751 she proceeded to lay out Clayton Square and the surrounding streets, many of which were named after family members and connections. This was one of the few attempts at formal town planning in Georgian Liverpool. This view shows the south east corner of the square, with Littlewoods' Café on the corner of Cases Street, the News Theatre Ltd. next door and Brown's, drapers, on the corner of Parker Street. *Binns Collection D425*

Cases Street, 1948

This view shows Cases Street, looking from Ranelagh Street towards Clayton Square, with Houghton Street in the distance. Today, although Cases Street still exists, it is much shorter and the view interrupted by the new Clayton Square shopping centre, opened 1988.
Binns Collection C201

Houghton Street, 1948

Houghton Street runs in a dog-leg from Clayton Square to Williamson Square and is named after one of Liverpool's early merchant families. All the shops on the right-hand side of the street were demolished in the late 1960s to make way for the new St John's Market and Precinct. St John's Beacon now stands at the bend in the road. On the left is Owen Owen's department store, founded by the Welshman Owen Owen in the 1860s. His first shop was situated in London Road and he gained a reputation for immaculate service and attractive window displays, which were a novelty in the 1870s. The store in Clayton Square opened in 1925, in a building originally intended as a hotel and is now a branch of Tesco Metro.

Binns Collection C200

Playhouse Theatre, 1954

The Playhouse Theatre was built as the New Star Music Hall, which opened in December 1866. The façade was still virtually unchanged when this picture was painted in 1954. In 1910 the theatre became the home of the Liverpool Repertory Company with the auditorium redesigned by Stanley D. Adshead. The building to the left, which looks like one of the original eighteenth century houses, was replaced in 1968 by an uncompromisingly modern extension. *Binns Collection B101*

Church Street, 1951

This view of Church Street looks eastwards from its junction with Williamson Street, towards Ranelagh Street and Central Station. A number of Liverpool's major shops were situated here and today it remains one of the city's important shopping streets. On the left are the twin towers of Compton House, originally established in 1832 as a small drapers, which expanded to occupy much of the land between Basnett Street and Tarleton Street. The building shown here was built after a disastrous fire in 1865, although the firm never recovered and the shop closed in 1871. Today the façade remains, minus the towers, and it has been a Marks and Spencer store since the 1930s. On the right is the canopy of C and A Modes Ltd., rebuilt in the 1980s and now occupied by Next.

Binns Collection C290

Ranelagh Street, 1947

This view looks along Ranelagh Street, towards Church Street, with the former Boots Chemist shop (originally the Bank of Liverpool) in the centre and Owen Owens, Clayton Square, on the right. Both Lewis's, from where this view is taken, and Blackler's department store, just out of shot to the right, were destroyed during the May Blitz and subsequently rebuilt on the same sites. This is one of two pictures by Tankard selected for exhibition at the Royal Academy in 1950. *Binns Collection C185*

Parker Street, 1947

Parker Street, on the left, is the short road linking Church Street with Clayton Square. The building in the centre of the picture, occupied by Broadbridge's opticians, was probably built about 1880 and has been incorporated into the new Clayton Square shopping centre. Central Station can be seen in the distance on the right. *Binns Collection C189*

Church Street, 1947

This view of Church Street, from Waterloo Place, at the junction of Hanover Street, looks towards Compton House, with its two towers. The shops on the right were obviously intended to attract a discerning clientele. There were two furriers (Soden Ltd., 'court furriers' and the Bankruptcy Fur Co Ltd.), and two jewellers (W. Wright Ltd. and Alfred Wolf Ltd.). The canopied shop to the right was the premises of John Bagshaw and Sons, 'silversmiths, jewellers, trunk and fitted travelling bag manufacturers, handbags and leather goods and fancy goods of all descriptions'. Next door were D.L. Phillips 'makers and designers of blouses, gowns, coats, costumes and knitwear'. When the Clayton Square shopping centre was built in the 1980s, these shops were retained, preserving just a little of Liverpool's old character.

Binns Collection C192

Bluecoat Chambers, 1959

Built as the Blue Coat Hospital or School in 1716/1717 this is the oldest building in the centre of Liverpool. The charity and its building were endowed by retired sea captain Bryan Blundell, who donated a portion of his income to the charity until his death in 1756. After the school moved to Wavertree in 1906 the building was acquired by Lord Leverhulme and in 1927 the newly formed Bluecoat Society of the Arts bought it from his executors. It was severely damaged by bombing in 1941, but restoration work had been completed by 1951, before this picture was painted. Tankard had a studio here for many years. *Local Collection 516*

Church Alley and Church Street, 1949

This picture, obviously painted on a showery day, with a double rainbow in the sky, looks across what was then open space from the Bluecoat Chambers towards Church Street. Marks and Spencer's can be seen on the left in the former Compton House and the building to the right is the Bon Marché, a high class ladies fashion store. This was opened in 1878 by David Lewis, the owner of Lewis's department store in Ranelagh Street, in imitation of the Paris store of the same name, even adopting the same colour scheme for his delivery vans and advertising. *Binns Collection C244*

College Lane, 1948

College Lane runs from Paradise Street to Hanover Street, at the rear of the Bluecoat Chambers. This view shows the remaining property from Peter's Lane, looking towards the bomb site of Hanover Street. A notice on the wall of the building on the right indicates that the Liverpool Ropery Co Ltd, whose premises had presumably been destroyed, have moved to Rathbone Road, Wavertree. However some businesses remain, including William Mooney and Sons Ltd., contractors and a sheet metal works. *Binns Collection C217*

Paradise Street, 1947

This view shows the east side of Paradise Street, from Church Street to School Lane. On the corner of Church Street is Cooper's provision merchants (with the scaffolding) with the Beehive public house, still there today and outwardly unchanged, to the right. The other businesses include Dents Ltd., dyers and cleaners, Blake's Medical Stores, surgical appliance dealers and the British Rawhide Belting Co. Ltd. The opposite side of the street has been demolished after bombing. On the corner of Whitechapel and Church Street is Bunney's Ltd., household stores and fancy goods dealers. *Binns Collection D433*

Paradise Street, 1947

This shows the large area devastated by enemy action on the south side of Lord Street, from Derby Square to Paradise Street. Looking towards the junction of Lord Street, Church Street, Paradise Street and Whitechapel, the twin spires of Bunney's household stores can be seen in the centre. On the opposite corner is Cooper's Stores, described in the 1949 Kelly's Directory of Liverpool as "grocers and tea dealers, provision, wine and spirit, tobacco and cigar, fancy goods, fruit, vegetables, meat and hardware merchants, ironmongers etc." and memorable to many Liverpudlians of a certain age, for the smell of fresh roasted coffee as one passed through the doors in Church Street.

Binns Collection C191

AROUND MOUNT PLEASANT

Mount Pleasant, 1947

Mount Pleasant is seen here from the Liverpool University School of Hygiene at the junction of Mount Pleasant and Oxford Street, looking towards Brownlow Hill, with the tower of the Victoria Building of the University in the distance. Behind the wall on the left is the site of the former Liverpool Workhouse, built in 1771 and rebuilt in the mid-nineteenth century. This was one of the largest workhouses in England, with accommodation for 4,000 inhabitants. The workhouse existed well into the twentieth century, although by then the emphasis had shifted to the care of the sick poor. *Binns Collection C194*

Mount Pleasant, 1947

This is another view of Mount Pleasant, this time looking from the grounds of the old Workhouse. In 1930 the land was purchased by the Archdiocese of Liverpool as the site for a new Roman Catholic, or Metropolitan, Cathedral for the city. Work began in 1933 to designs by Edward Lutyens, but only the crypt of what would have been a massive building, was completed before World War II intervened. Work on the newly commissioned, distinctive, circular cathedral designed by Frederick Gibberd did not start until 1959.

Binns Collection C195

Mount Pleasant, 1948

This view shows the south side of Mount Pleasant, with Roscoe Street in the centre. The house to the left with the brick archway (number 68) was built about 1788 for the merchant George Dunbar, and at the time the picture was painted it formed part of the Liverpool Chest Hospital. On the far right is the YMCA, built 1874-1877 in "thirteenth century Gothic style." The houses between include the oldest in the street (number 62), built in 1767 for another merchant, William Rice. By 1948 these had been split into numerous offices, with the Registry Office for the south of the city at number 64. *Binns Collection C227*

Mount Pleasant, 1948

The terrace houses on the north side of Mount Pleasant were built slightly later, around 1800 and by the 1940s many had been converted into small hotels, some of which survive today. They included a number of temperance hotels, such as the Douglas Temperance Hotel (number 47), the Adelphi Temperance Hotel (number 59) and the Albion Temperance Hotel (number 53, with an annexe at number 35). The Adelphi Hotel, not to be confused with the temperance hotel of the same name, can be seen in the distance.
Binns Collection C228

Mount Pleasant, 1951

This building is the former Mount Pleasant Methodist Chapel, built 1790. By the date of this painting it had become a Public Billiard Hall, proprietor Frank Woods and in later years it was the Mardi Gras jazz club. The poster on the left of the building advertises the Turner and Sons Century Auction Galleries, who had premises next door. To the right, on the gable wall, is another poster advertising the optician Albert E. Walsby, at 21 and 23 Mount Pleasant. *Binns Collection C285*

Brownlow Hill, 1947

Brownlow Hill was one of the old routes out of Liverpool and on Eyes' map of the town in 1768 it is labelled as the "road to Warrington", but it was not until the early nineteenth century that it started to be built up. On the left is the Adelphi Hotel, built 1911-1914 and the third hotel of that name on the site. In the eighteenth century, before any of the hotels were built it was the site of Ranelagh Gardens, named after the London gardens of the same name. Entertainments provided there included firework displays, jugglers and concerts; tea and other refreshments, including "strawberries buttered with crème", were served.

Binns Collection C187

**Victoria Building,
Liverpool University, 1949**

The Victoria Building, built 1887 to 1892, was designed by Alfred Waterhouse for the University College, before it became the University of Liverpool. This "stridently red and assertively Gothic" building is the epitome of a "red-brick university" and the clock tower and corner turret are landmarks on Brownlow Hill. The building was designed to be fireproof, with an iron frame and concrete floors and housed a library and lecture theatre. *Binns Collection C243*

Liverpool University, 1949

This quadrangle is the open space at the rear of the Victoria Building. On the left is the Ashton Building, built for the Faculty of Arts in 1912-1914. Its classical design, derived from the work of Christopher Wren, forms a striking contrast with Waterhouse's red-brick Gothic. *Binns Collection C246*

Hope Street, 1950

Hope Street takes its name from William Hope, who built and lived in a house at the corner of Hardman Street. This row of Georgian houses, numbers 60 to 66, is on the west side of the street, between Rice Street, on the right and Mount Street, on the left. The larger, double fronted house in the centre was the 'Private Chauffeurs' Club' when the picture was painted and is now the restaurant '60 Hope Street.'

Binns Collection C271

Hope Street, 1947

Another view from the old Workhouse, looking along Hope Street, towards the Anglican Cathedral. On the left is the colonnaded building of the Liverpool Medical Institution. Built in 1837 at a cost of £4,000, it housed the medical library established by doctors at the Liverpool Infirmary. The building also provided a meeting place for members of the medical profession. Next to the Medical Institution is Hope Hall, built as the Hope Chapel in 1837. It opened as the Hope Hall Cinema in 1912 and in 1964 it became the Everyman Theatre. On the opposite corner is the Catholic convent of Notre Dame, which also included a school and training college for female teachers. It is now part of Liverpool John Moores University.

Binns Collection C196

Radium Institute, Myrtle Street, 1948

The Radium Institute was founded in Islington in 1862 as the Hospital for Cancer and Skin Diseases. It moved to premises in Myrtle Street in 1882, which had formerly been the Lying-in Hospital, built in 1861. The tall building to the rear is the first phase of a planned new hospital, opened in 1933, but never completed. In the mid-1960s facilities were moved to Clatterbridge Hospital on the Wirral. *Binns Collection C209*

Philharmonic Hall, 1954

The Liverpool Philharmonic Society held its first concert in 1840 and is the second oldest music and concert promoting society in the country. In 1849 the Society built its own concert hall in Hope Street, designed by John Cunningham. In 1933 a fire disastrously destroyed the building, although the new hall, in art-deco style, designed by Herbert J. Rowse, opened only six years later. To the right is Hope Street Unitarian Church.

Binns Collection C291

Rodney Street, 1945

The Anglican Cathedral can be seen in the distance in this view of the southern part of Rodney Street, from its junction with Hardman Street. This is one of Liverpool's most architecturally striking streets, laid out by William Roscoe and others 1783-4, although only gradually developed up to the 1820s. On the right-hand side, at number 62, is the house built for John Gladstone in 1792-3 where his son William Ewart Gladstone, the orator, poet, scholar and statesman, was born in 1809. This is one of two Tankard pictures selected for exhibition at the Royal Academy in 1950.

Binns Collection D391

Rodney Street, 1945

This view looks in the opposite direction, along the northern section of the street. Despite its apparent uniformity the houses were developed piecemeal and are all of slightly different design; some have five bays, others three and there are varying styles of doorways and porches. Rodney Street was developed for Liverpool 'gentlemen' wishing to live outside the noisy, congested centre of town, but in time it became Liverpool's equivalent of Harley Street as doctors, dentists and other medical professionals opened consulting rooms there; in Kelly's Liverpool Directory for 1949 virtually every house lists medical practitioners. *Binns Collection D392*

St Andrew's Church, Rodney Street, 1948

St Andrew's Church stands on the east side of Rodney Street, close to its junction with Mount Pleasant. Built for the Scottish Presbyterians, it opened on 3rd December 1824, with a sermon by the then famous Rev. Edward Irving, who was admired "for his talents and character, with a little criticism for his extravagance and peculiarities." Today this fine building has been derelict for a number of years as arguments over its future use and restoration continue.

Binns Collection C222

HANOVER STREET
TO THE ANGLICAN CATHEDRAL

Hanover Street, 1947

In the eighteenth century Hanover Street was one of Liverpool's most important streets. Many of the expanding town's merchants built houses there, with their names recalled in the streets and buildings of the locality, such as Seel Street (after Thomas Seel), Blackburne House and School (after John Blackburne) and Colquitt Street (after John Colquitt). This view shows the Hanover Hotel, a much altered survival from the eighteenth century, looking towards Bold Street on the far left. *Binns Collection C186*

Hanover Street and Seel Street, 1950

This view vividly illustrates the destruction caused by World War II bombing and probably shows the junction of Hanover Street and Seel Street, looking eastwards towards the Anglican Cathedral, although with so few landmarks remaining it is difficult to be precise. A notice on the remains of the building to the left indicates that Baxendale and Co Ltd., sanitary engineers, builders' merchants, ironmongers and paint manufacturers, are now trading in what appears to be Monument Place. *Binns Collection C267*

Bridewell, Argyle Street, 1950

Argyle Street was named after John, Duke of Argyle, celebrated by Sir Walter Scott in his novel "Heart of Midlothian" with the area being laid out in the mid-eighteenth century. The Old Bridewell, shown here, was built in 1861 as police cells and offices and has now, somewhat surprisingly, been converted into a restaurant. *Binns Collection C269*

Slater Street, 1949

Slater Street runs from Duke Street to Bold Street, intersecting Seel Street and Wood Street at right-angles and is shown here looking towards Bold Street, at its junction with Parr Street. On the left is the Cumberland Arms, licensee Mrs Catherine Fasting and at the time of this painting there were a number of small manufacturers in the street, making, amongst other things, gas mantles, cash tills, caps, ladders and ladder attachments. There was a ticket writer, an antique repairer and an antique furniture dealer, a gold beater, as well as a firm of artists' colourmen. *Binns Collection D450*

Bold Street, 1945

Until World War II Bold Street was Liverpool's most exclusive shopping area. On the right are the premises of Sloan Ltd, who dealt in "Modes, robes, Tailleurs fourrures [fur coats] and lingerie." Beyond, on the opposite corner of Concert Street, is the much altered Concert Hall of 1785/6 originally capable of seating 1400, with an orchestra of 150. Shops were later created on the ground floor, with a concert hall above; more recently it formed the premises of Waterstones bookshop. In the distance the tower of St Luke's Church is just visible. After they were bombed out of their store in Great Charlotte Street in 1941 Blackler's occupied no less than eleven different shops in Bold Street, with the various different departments split between them. *Local Collection 303*

Renshaw Street, 1951

In the mid-eighteenth century, like most roads leading from the centre of town Renshaw Street was just a rural lane. To one side was one of the town's many ropery works, supplying rope for ships' rigging in the expanding port. A number of prominent places of worship, of various persuasions, were later situated in this road, including a Unitarian Chapel, an Independent Chapel and an Episcopal Church. The bombed out remains of St Luke's Church of England Church still stand at the far end, where the road joins with Bold Street and Hardman Street. In this 1951 view the only religious building remaining on Renshaw Street is the Central Hall, the prominent building in the centre of the picture. *Binns Collection C286*

Panorama, 1950

This panoramic view from the top of Lewis's, looks south-east along Renshaw Street. In the distance is the tower of St Luke's Church at the top of Bold Street and to the right is the unmistakeable shape of the Anglican Cathedral. In the bottom right-hand corner is the cutting of

Central Station, still with steam trains at this date. Renshaw Street runs diagonally from the bottom-left of the painting, with Central Hall and its array of domes, the most prominent building. Opened in 1905 by the Liverpool

Wesleyan Mission as a centre for concerts and social activities, as well as a place of worship, it was used as a nightclub for a number of years. *Binns Collection A59*

107

Colquitt Street, 1947

This view of Colquitt Street shows some of the devastation caused by air raids during World War II. The Apothecaries' Hall stood at the corner of Colquitt Street and Wood Street and had been rebuilt in a fireproof design following a fire in 1846. As can be seen the building, including a stone façade surviving from the original, suffered severe damage. However the remaining warehouse has recently been converted into flats. *Binns Collection D432*

Seel Street, 1949

This picture shows the top end of Seel Street, from its junction with Back Berry Street, looking towards Berry Street. The street is named after Thomas Seel who, in the mid-eighteenth century owned a large mansion in Hanover Street, with extensive gardens and grounds. At the end of the eighteenth century the street was cut through this land and the area laid out in building plots. The houses shown here obviously date from that period, with their pedimented doors and bow-fronted shop windows. On the left is Smith's Cooperage Ltd. and the window of Thomas Yates Price, fried fish dealer, advertises 'Fresh fried fish' and 'The tastiest, crispest chips in town.'

Binns Collection D447

Mount Street, 1950

Tankard must have known this street well. On the left is Liverpool College of Art, where he was a student and taught for many years. This part was built in 1882 and designed by Thomas Cook. The building with the imposing columns beyond was built as the Liverpool Mechanics' Institution in 1835-1837 and later developed into the Liverpool Institute High School for boys. After the school closed in the 1990s the building found a new use as Liverpool Institute of Performing Arts. On the opposite side of the road is a row of Georgian houses which still stand today. *Binns Collection C268*

Blackburne House, 1947

John Blackburne, Mayor of Liverpool in 1788, built Blackburne House between 1785 and 1790, in what was then countryside on a hill outside the town and the grounds extended from Falkner Street to Blackburne Place. When a female branch of the Mechanics Institute was established in 1844 George Holt, a local merchant and philanthropist, purchased the house in memory of his daughter, to provide premises for the organisation, which later became the Liverpool Institute High School for Girls. The portico and staircase hall of the original house survive, although the building has been much added to over the years. In 1994 after the school had closed, it was converted for use as a women's training centre.
Binns Collection D430.

Upper Duke Street, 1949

This is Upper Duke Street looking downhill towards Duke Street and the Liver Building in the distance, from the junction with Roscoe Street. On the right hand side, originally the site of St Martin's Church, is the warehouse of Lewis's department store, which later became Liverpool Music Library. The shop on the left was a tobacconist, run by Rose Bradley, now demolished and replaced by the Dean Walters Building of Liverpool John Moores University.

Binns Collection C236

Anglican Cathedral, 1951

Work on Liverpool's Anglican Cathedral started in 1904, but was not completed until 1978. The Gothic design, by Sir Giles Gilbert Scott, was the result of a competition in 1901 won by Scott when he was only 22 years old, although his original design was later much amended. The Lady Chapel, the first part to be completed and seen here on the left, was consecrated in 1910. Work on the east side began first and the Cathedral appears complete when seen in this view from Hope Street. However, work on the nave, at the north west end and out of sight, continued from 1948 to 1978. The site, on a sandstone ridge above the former St James' Quarry and Cemetery, south of the city centre, ensures that the Cathedral is a dominant feature on the city skyline. *Binns Collection C288*

Anglican Cathedral, 1949

This view of the west front of the Cathedral shows that work is still very much underway. The Rankin Porch in the centre appears complete, but the nave, on the far left, has yet to be built and would not be completed until 30 years after this picture was painted. Scott's competition winning design envisaged twin towers, but this was modified and replaced with a larger, single central tower. Eighteenth century housing occupied the sloping land in front of the Cathedral, but as can be seen here, it suffered from bomb damage, although the area would not be redeveloped until the 1980s.
Binns Collection C315

LIVERPOOL MANSIONS

Croxteth Hall, 1959

In the early eighteenth century Croxteth Hall became the main home of William 4th Viscount Molyneux, and work commenced on the Queen Anne Wing, shown here, transforming a modest house into an imposing mansion. The family fortunes rose even higher in 1771 when the 8th Viscount was created 1st Earl of Sefton. During the nineteenth century Croxteth evolved into a well run country estate, supplying the needs of the hall and its many guests, as well as the estate workers. In 1952, before this picture was painted, a fire caused serious damage to the Queen Anne wing, and although not obvious from the outside, many of the rooms have never been restored. *Local Collection 521*

Croxteth Hall, 1959

A view of the servants' quarters, this picture shows the stable yard, with a pump and trough in the centre. In 1972 the 7th Earl, Hugh William Osbert Molyneux, died without an heir and the title became extinct. The contents of the hall, including the pictures, furniture and library, were sold the following year. Today the house and grounds are run by Liverpool City Council as a visitor attraction.

Local Collection 519

May Place, Broadgreen, 1945

May Place, a large detached red-brick house, was built in the eighteenth century and still stands in Broadgreen Road. According to James Hoult, historian of Old Swan, the builder of the house was an African slave-trader who married an Indian princess. Over the centuries it has been the home of Mr Papayanni, a shipowner, Mr Spence, a Methodist sympathiser, and a Mr Austin, who was alleged to have had 20 children. For some years it was a school run by Rev Wilson, later a Catholic Reformatory for girls and then St Vincent's Hospice for the Dying. Today it is part of a sheltered housing complex. *Binns Collection C175*

The Grange, Edge Lane, 1949

This house was built in 1830 by James Ryley, a Liverpool cotton broker and stood on Edge Lane, at its junction with Botanic Road. In 1900 it became the headquarters of the 4th West Lancashire Medium Regiment (359th) and a drill hall was constructed on land behind the house. In 1951 it was demolished and replaced by a modern building. *Binns Collection C247*

The Hazels, Prescot, 1950

This house was built in the Palladian style in 1764 and later belonged to the Pilkington family. In 1945 it opened as a teacher training college for women, named after C.F. Mott, the former Director of Education in Liverpool, and later became Liverpool College of Higher Education. The site is now being redeveloped as a business park. *Binns Collection C273*

Penny Lane, 1948

This house was known as Grove House when painted by Tankard in 1948 and dates back to at least 1836. In the 1870s the owner A.G. Kurtz, an alkali manufacturer and art collector, instructed C.Z. Hermann, a local architect to carry out alterations. However he was less than happy with the result, commenting that "I felt rather sorry that I have had it altered." It later became a public house named Dovedale Towers.

Binns Collection C223

The Mount, Elmswood Road, 1951

This is one of a number of similar houses built in the Mossley Hill area by nineteenth century merchants and businessmen. The Mount stood at the junction of Elmswood Road and Woodlands Road. From 1851 to the mid-1870s the house was occupied by Edgar Garston and his family. A general merchant, born in Chester, the family firm, E. and J.H. Garston and Co. had offices in Rumford Place in the centre of Liverpool. The family were reasonably affluent, as in 1871 they were able to employ a cook, a housemaid and a coachman, all of whom lived in. In 1861 they had a governess for their daughter Ethel Mary Garston. *Binns Collection C280*

Sudley, Mossley Hill Road, 1948

Sudley was built in c.1820 and became the residence of the shipowner, George Holt, from 1883 until his death. He enlarged and remodelled the house, adding tiled fireplaces, inlaid mahogany bookcases, an iron veranda on the garden front, with views of the river and a conservatory with 'Chinese glazing.' He was an avid collector of contemporary paintings and sculpture, reflecting Victorian tastes. His daughter, Emma Holt bequeathed the house and his collection to the city of Liverpool in 1944 and it now forms part of the National Museums Liverpool. *Binns Collection C225*

Carnatic Hall, 1947

Carnatic Hall in Elmswood Road, Mossley Hill, is now the site of Liverpool University halls of residence. The hall was built by Peter Baker in the late eighteenth century with the proceeds of his activities as a privateer. His ship, the 'Mentor', captured an unarmed French East Indiaman, the 'Carnatic', in 1778, with a cargo which included a box of diamonds valued between £135,00 and £400,000. His house at Mossley Hill was subsequently nicknamed 'Carnatic Hall' by local wits, although the name does not appear to have been formally used until 1889. During World War II Liverpool Museum used the house for storage of exhibits away from the city centre. *Binns Collection C193*

Woolton Hall, 1950

The present Woolton Hall was built for Richard Molyneux in the early eighteenth century, although there had been a building on the site for many years. In 1772 Nicholas Ashton, a Liverpool gentleman, with interests in canals, salt and shipping, bought the house. He commissioned the famous architect, Robert Adam, to remodel the interior and this is probably the only example of his work in Lancashire, including the cantilevered staircase shown here. The hall now stands in the grounds of St Julie's Roman Catholic School. In 1974 an application to demolish it as surplus to requirements was vigorously opposed and following restoration work it is now used as function rooms.

Binns Collection C260

Speke Hall, 1955

Speke Hall is a remarkable survivor, approached through the industrial suburbs of south Liverpool, it is one of four important timber-framed buildings in the north of England. Built by the Catholic Norris family, it reached its present form in 1598 under Edward Norris. In 1795 Richard Watt, a local West India merchant, purchased the near derelict building. He and his descendants, especially Richard Watt V in the mid-nineteenth century, carried out extensive restoration work on the hall. The last owner, Adelaide Watt, bequeathed Speke Hall to the National Trust on her death on 1921.

This view shows the north front, with its distinctive black timbers and white plaster work, although it is thought that the tar compound with which the timbers were treated was only applied in the nineteenth century.
Binns Collection C294

Speke Hall, 1955

The central courtyard of Speke Hall was built in phases over at least 200 years and completed in 1598. Until the nineteenth century the main entrance to the house would have been via the moat bridge, shown in the previous view, through the gatehouse and across the courtyard. In the courtyard stand two magnificent yew trees, named Adam and Eve, one of which can be seen here.

Binns Collection C298

THE SUBURBS

Everton, 1949

This aerial view of Everton looks from the roof of Penrhyn Street School, off Great Homer Street, up the hill towards Northumberland Terrace and St George's Hill. The road leading straight up the hill is Beatrice Street, with the newsagent's shop of Isabella McGuiness on the corner of Great Homer Street. The public house on the left is the Old Grapes Inn. This picture shows the damage caused by air raids, where houses have been cleared from Beatrice Street to Anthony Street, on the right and further up the hill towards Northumberland Terrace.

Binns Collection C231

Everton Terrace, 1949

In the late eighteenth and early nineteenth centuries the higher ground at Everton was a favoured place of residence for Liverpool merchants who wanted to leave the congestion of the town. A number of villas were built on the east side of Everton Terrace, with extensive views towards the town, with the River Mersey, Liverpool Bay and the Welsh mountains beyond. Gradually these villas were replaced by terrace housing and this picture shows one of the few remaining villas, which in 1949 formed part of Heyworth Street County Primary School.
Binns Collection C229

St George's Hill, 1949

St George's Hill (formerly called Hill Side) ran uphill from the end of Everton Terrace. By the end of the nineteenth century this area was covered in rows of terrace housing. In 1948 typical occupations of the residents of St George's Hill were dock worker, labourer, railway guard, tram conductor and storekeeper. In the 1960s much of this property was demolished as part of the city's slum clearance programme. Today the land between Netherfield Road and Heyworth Street is open parkland.

Binns Collection C230

St Francis Xavier Church, Salisbury Street, 1949

The Roman Catholic Church of St Francis Xavier formed part of Liverpool's largest group of ecclesiastical buildings. The church was designed by J.J. Scoles of London in an Early English Gothic style and opened in 1848. The tower, detached from the main body of the church, is topped by a recessed spire, which was not added until 1883. The Sodality Chapel, to the right of the tower, was built 1885-1887 by Edmund Kirby and houses the altars of a number of sodalities or pious lay associations. To the right of the church is the College, now part of Liverpool Hope University and beyond that are the secondary schools.

Binns Collection C248

Low Hill, 1950

Low Hill was one of the earliest settled areas outside the centre of Liverpool. The name is of Danish origin, 'low' indicating a tumulus or burial mound. This view looks along Kensington, with the Coach and Horses public house on the left. Until 1835 this was the boundary of the town of Liverpool and the open space in front of the public house was associated with the tradition of 'beating the bounds', a ceremony attended by the Mayor and Corporation officials. A procession 'marked' the northern boundaries, and then stopped for lunch at Low Hill. An account of the 1800 event tells of a lunch, including pigeon pies, hams, fowls, brandy, rum and wine, served at a cost of £16 9s 6d (£16.47). After lunch the southern boundaries were less diligently 'beaten' and the custom died out after 1835 when the boundaries were extended. *Binns Collection C256*

Glass works.   Detaild Dwg   Half the Square – Albert Road.

Albert Road, Edge Hill, 1950

This terrace of houses is situated just south of the Edge Hill railway sidings, off Spekeland Road, each house being built at the end of long garden, around what was in effect a quadrangle.

This view shows the east side, numbers 43 to 63, numbered consecutively. By 1950 they were inhabited by labourers, plasterers, gardeners,

carters, railway employees etc. The chimneys to the left belong to the glass bottle manufacturers Bateson Brothers. *Binns Collection C254*

Albert Road, Edge Hill, 1950

A close-up of two of the houses in Albert Road, identified by Tankard as numbers 42 and 43, showing the attractive entrance porches of each house. According the Kelly's Liverpool Directory and Tankard's note on the picture, number 42 is the Spekefield Inn, landlord Dominck Mulloy, although it looks more like a private house.
Binns Collection C255

East Prescot Road, 1950

These two pictures, when joined together, form a panoramic view of numbers 204 to 266 East Prescot Road, with the numbers running from right to left. The large building on the left is the Knotty Ash Hotel, run by Mrs Florence May Jump.

The archway between numbers 240 and 242 leads to the picturesquely named Little Bongs.
Binns Collection C249

Little Bongs, 1950

Little Bongs is a small group of cottages, built by a local brewery, which still exist, secluded behind the cottages fronting onto East Prescot Road. Their name is something of a mystery and suggestions for its origin range from the old field name, the bungs used in brewers' casks or from the word 'bong', meaning a bank. This view looks back towards the arched entrance from East Prescot Road, with the cottages on the left.

Binns Collection C253

East Prescot Road, 1950

This is another view of East Prescot Road, looking westwards from the junction with Thomas Lane. Both this picture and previous views of East Prescot Road have been annotated by the artist, with the house numbers and shop names, which must have been familiar to him as he lived in the area. The detached house in the centre of the picture, at number 256, belonged to Thomas Sowerby and Son, who must have been some of the last dairy farmers in Liverpool, delivering milk locally from their own herd of cows, which grazed on land near St Edward's Orphanage. Just beyond is the shop of Miss Elizabeth Ann Baskett, confectioner and further along is Edward Stanley Baskett's newsagent shop. *Binns Collection C251*

Railway Cottages, Old Thomas Lane, 1950

These four cottages stood close to the rear entrance to Broadgreen Station and the canopy roof of the station can just be seen to the right. Tankard lived close by in Thomas Lane at the time of his marriage. Old Thomas Lane was formed when Thomas Lane was straightened to provide a direct connection with the bridge under the railway to Bowring Park Road. The two-up two-down cottages were demolished in the 1950s and it is now the site of the Jehovah's Witnesses' Kingdom Hall. *Binns Collection C258*

Dudlow Road Pumping Station, 1951

This pumping station, owned by Liverpool Corporation Water Works, was built in the 1860s to help satisfy Liverpool's increasing demand for water. The red sandstone tower formed a prominent local landmark until its demolition, shown here. The 275 feet well, with two shafts and boreholes at the base could pump up to one million gallons of water each day. There were also a number of reservoirs on the site and a row of five cottages for water company employees.

Binns Collection C284

Mossley Hill Church, 1949

The church of St Matthew and St James was funded by a legacy from a 1830s visitor to Mossley Hill and dedicated to the saints after whom he was named. Designed by Paley and Austin of Lancaster and consecrated in 1875, its early parishioners consisted of wealthy merchants and their servants, from the nearby big houses, in what was then a sparsely populated area. In the twentieth century this changed as the surrounding fields were gradually covered with houses. Although not obvious in this view, the church was severely damaged and the original stained glass by Morris and Co. destroyed in one of Liverpool's first air raids in August 1940. Situated on a ridge, 188 feet above sea level the church tower is still a prominent landmark. *Binns Collection C238*

Mayfair Hotel, Park Lane, 1950

This ornate public house, situated at the junction of Park Lane and Sparling Street, has a distinct nautical flavour, with mythical figures, including Neptune (with trident) on the parapet and urns, dolphins, shells, ships and anchors. It appears to have been built almost by mistake; there were plans to extend the railway from Edge Hill to Park Lane and the brewery, anticipating the extra trade that this would bring, had the Mayfair Hotel built. Unfortunately the line was only for goods traffic! In Kelly's Directory it is listed at number 172, despite having the number 168 prominently carved on the corner. The hotel later became known as the Excelsior and finally Kean's Hotel, before its demolition in the 1980s.

Binns Collection C272

Further reading

Aughton, Peter *Liverpool: a people's history*. Carnegie Publishing, rev. ed. 2003.

Sharples, Joseph Liverpool, Pevsner Architectural Guides, Yale University Press, 2004.

Pollard, Richard and Nikolaus Pevsner *Lancashire: Liverpool and the south-west, The Buildings of England*, Yale University Press, 2006.

Picton, J.A. *Memorials of Liverpool: historical and topographical, 2 vols.*, Longmans, Green and Co, London, 2nd ed. 1875.

Bradbury, R. *Liverpool builds, 1945-65*. Liverpool City Council, 1965.